Viking Feast

Medieval Banquet

Roman Saturnalia

Greek Festival of Wine

First World War Christmas

Egyptian Dinner Party

Mammoth Meal

Indian Wedding

ASIA

AFRICA

INDIAN OCEAN

AUSTRALIA

Peter Kent's Wide-Eyed World

FABULOUS
FEASTS

MACDONALD YOUNG BOOKS

Wide-Eyed World of Literacy

You can use this book as a literacy resource to:
identify a range of information text elements including headings,
lists, bullet points and paragraphs

●

identify features of an instructional text, for example lists of
ingredients

●

retrieve information accessibly via a comprehensive contents list,
page numbers, glossary and index

●

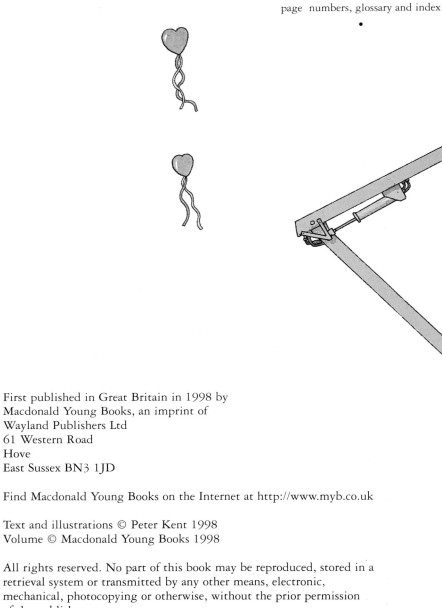

First published in Great Britain in 1998 by
Macdonald Young Books, an imprint of
Wayland Publishers Ltd
61 Western Road
Hove
East Sussex BN3 1JD

Find Macdonald Young Books on the Internet at http://www.myb.co.uk

Text and illustrations © Peter Kent 1998
Volume © Macdonald Young Books 1998

A CIP catalogue for this book is available from
the British Library

ISBN 0 7500 2526 3

Editor: Lisa Edwards
Designer: Sally Downes
Illustrator: Peter Kent

Printed and bound in Portugal by Edições ASA

Contents

A Mammoth Meal

8000 BC

Stone Age people got their food by hunting wild animals and gathering wild plants that were good to eat. Animals then were much larger and fiercer than animals today. There were savage sabre-toothed tigers, giant beavers and enormous deer. Largest of all was the great woolly mammoth; it was like a huge, hairy elephant.

Menu
Can you find –

·

A mammoth being pushed off a cliff

·

A dog eating a mammoth steak

·

7 gut sausages (brains and liver mixed with fat and sewn up in a length of intestine)

·

A woman carrying a bowl of wild berries and fruits

·

Hunting these vast beasts was difficult and dangerous. People only had spears and arrows tipped with sharp stones to kill the animals. It needed extra courage and cunning to kill a mammoth. The best way was to force it over a cliff.

Once the mammoth was dead the tribe of hunters would celebrate. The huge carcass gave them tonnes of meat, lots of hairy hide for warm clothes and bedding, and bones and ivory to make tools. It was a good day for the tribe when they made a kill.

Guzzling Guests

Can you spot -

·

The Chief, wearing a horned headdress

·

The Shaman, wearing a leopardskin

·

A selfish person who won't share his mammoth steak

·

9 vultures waiting to eat the leftovers

·

An Egyptian Dinner Party

1500 BC

The Ancient Egyptians loved dinner parties. They wore their finest clothes, elaborate wigs and lots of make-up. The people giving the party greeted their guests at the door. Servants offered them garlands of flowers and cones of perfume to put on their heads.

The food was arranged in mouth-watering heaps and servants brought it to the guests. Sometimes the guests ate and drank so much they were sick, but no one minded.

Menu
Can you find -

- 3 ducks

- A boiled ox's head served with fruit

- 4 roast chickens in front of 4 greedy guests

- 2 servant girls carrying jars of wine on their heads

Musicians played during the meal and dancers, acrobats, conjurors and jugglers performed. When the party was over, servants arrived to carry away the guests who had drunk too much wine.

Guzzling Guests

Can you spot -

·

5 slaves holding ostrich-feather fans

·

2 acrobats bending over backwards

·

2 children allowed to stay up late

·

2 pet cats

·

A Greek Festival of Wine 400 BC

In Ancient Greece, dinner parties were for men only. Men and women feasted together only at public festivals. Every spring there were several days of feasting and drinking in honour of the new wine on sale for the first time. A statue of Dionysus, the god of wine, was carried to his temple. Everyone tasted the new wine, sang and danced.

Menu

Can you find -

•

2 plates of fried fish

•

a bull being led to the altar as a gift to the god of wine

•

A bowl of 11 orange pomegranates

•

A golden goblet

•

During the festival all children who had reached the age of three were given a special jug of wine. This showed they were not thought of as babies any more. On the last day of the festival, each family made a special meal for the spirits of their dead relatives and took it to the cemetery.

Guzzling Guests

Can you spot -

·

A discus thrower

·

a dog eating a joint
of roast mutton

·

A child sitting on his father's shoulders,
watching the procession

·

A Roman Saturnalia
AD 200

In December, the Romans had a festival called Saturnalia to honour the god Saturn. Everyone had a holiday and every family cooked a special meal. Slaves were allowed to dress in their masters' clothes and do what they liked. At the meal, the masters waited on the slaves.

Roman dinner parties were famous for their unusual menus and the vast amounts of food. The guests lay on couches round a low table.

Menu

Can you find -

·

A hare

·

A pig stuffed with sausages and blood puddings

·

5 mice served on a round plate

·

5 piglets made from pastry

·

There were no knives and forks so the Romans ate with their right hands – it was very bad manners to use the left hand.

During the meal, musicans, dancers, clowns and gladiators amused the guests. Greedy Romans had rooms in their houses where they could be sick to make room for more food.

Guzzling Guests

Can you spot -

·

2 gladiators carrying swords and shields

·

A child riding in a small chariot, drawn by two geese

·

A dancer wearing a yellow dress

·

A juggler who can't juggle

15

A Viking Supper
850

The Vikings loved feasting. A Viking chief wanted his followers to think he was generous as well as brave. The chief and his warriors would eat and drink together in the chief's hall and pass the time singing and telling stories of great deeds.

This picture shows a feast in a great hall called Heorot. It was the home of King Hrothgar, King of the Danes. This hall was cursed by a monster called Grendel who would break in while the warriors slept, carry them off to his lair and then eat them.

Menu
Can you find -

•

A serving girl carrying
7 fish on a tray

•

A boy giving a dog a bone

•

A sword stuck in a joint of
roast venison

•

10 pigs' trotters

•

Hrothgar despaired and begged the hero Beowulf to help. Beowulf agreed and came to Heorot. As he slept in the hall with fourteen warriors in full armour, Grendel burst in the door and ate one of them.

Beowulf awoke and grabbed Grendel's scaly arm and pulled until he tore it from the monster's shoulder. Grendel staggered back to his lair and died. Beowulf tied Grendel's arm to a beam in the hall.

Guzzling Guests

Can you spot –

Beowulf showing someone how he pulled the monster's arm until it came off

Ragnor Hairy-Trousers, fast asleep

A Skald, or poet, with his harp

Five dogs

A Medieval Banquet
1400

During the Middle Ages, a great lord would eat his meals in public every day, but on special occasions he would have a banquet. The lord sat with his family and very special guests on a raised platform. Everybody else sat at long tables.

Serving the meal was very complicated and needed lots of servants. There was one servant who brought water for hand-washing, another brought bread rolls, a butler who was in charge of drinks, a carver, cup-bearer and chief cook. There was also a taster, just in case anyone had poisoned the food.

Menu
Can you find -
•

A swan wearing a crown

•

A boiled chicken, stuffed with purple grapes

•

8 custard pies on a large tray

•

a barrel of beer

•

The guests used knives to cut their food but ate with their fingers. Instead of plates they had trenchers, which were slices of stale bread. At the end of the meal, these were given to poor, starving people.

Guzzling Guests

Can you spot -

·

7 musicians

·

The court jester, with bells on his hat

·

2 small kitchen boys, wearing aprons

·

The chief cook, wearing his gold chain of office

·

An Aztec Feast
1500

The Aztecs, who lived in what is now Mexico, were a very warlike people. Every man had to join the army and if he was brave he was rewarded with clothes, slaves and land. An especially brave man was made a knight. The Aztecs had three sorts of knight: Jaguar knights, Arrow knights and Eagle knights. This picture shows a feast given by an Aztec nobleman to celebrate his son becoming a knight.

Aztecs had no cows or sheep so they ate very little meat. Mostly they ate thin corn cakes called tortillas. At a feast they ate more elaborate and unusual foods. Tamales were corn 'envelopes' stuffed with such delights as frogs, snails, insect eggs and worms.

There was music and dancing at Aztec feasts, but the musicians had to be careful. If they played out of tune they were fined.

Guzzling Guests

Can you spot -

6 Jaguar knights

A child wearing a Jaguar headdress

2 real jaguars

4 nobles wearing feather cloaks

Menu

Can you find -

An Eagle knight with a
cup of cactus beer

A turtle

A parrot hiding behind a
jar of drinking chocolate

10 crabs

An Indian Wedding
1650

The Indian Raja Viraballala gave a magnificent feast to celebrate the marriage of his daughter Rajadhiraja to the King of Veni. The feast was so wonderful that minstrels sang about it for fifty years. A new dining hall was built on an island in an artificial lake. It was hung with gorgeous silk curtains and tapestries.

Menu
Can you find -

- **2 swordfish**
- **4 turtles baked in their shells**
- **2 peacocks stuffed with almonds**
- **A roast ostrich**

All the best cooks in southern India were ordered to create the most mouthwatering dishes for the feast. A servant was even sent 3200km to get just one rare spice. A special water cart was built to transport exotic fish from the coast to the palace.

Three thousand guests were invited to Raja Viraballala's feast. They were entertained with acrobats, clowns, dancers, musicians, magicians and storytellers. The guests enjoyed it so much they refused to leave and the Raja sent his soldiers to force them home.

Guzzling Guests

Can you spot -

- A snake charmer
- 6 fan-bearers
- A pet leopard
- 7 monkeys
- A fakir climbing a rope in the air

A Barn Dance
1880

In nineteenth-century America, the pioneers who settled in the west had to help each other with setting up their farms. They could not afford to hire workers to do it for them. When a family settled on their new land, they needed a barn to store their crops.

All their neighbours joined together to help them. While the men worked on building the frame of the barn, the women prepared a delicious supper.

Menu
Can you find -
·
A cat helping herself to baked beans
·
A dog eating a grilled chop
·
A woman carrying a large apple pie
·
2 men eating sausages
·

The frame was hoisted up, fixed together and the roof and sides were nailed on. Then everybody went into the new barn, put up trestle tables and sat down to eat supper. After they'd eaten there would be a dance to the music of fiddles and accordions with a caller shouting out the dance steps for everybody to follow.

Guzzling Guests
Can you spot -
•

A girl who has stolen a guest's false teeth

•

A dancer stepping on his partner's feet

•

A baby who has eaten half an apple pie

•

a cat chasing a mouse

•

A Front Line Christmas
1914

During the First World War, the German army fought the French, Belgian and British armies from trenches dug across northern France. The soldiers were cold and wet. Their families sent them warm clothes and parcels of food.

On Christmas Day 1914, the two armies stopped fighting. They sang carols and climbed out of their trenches to meet one another. They swapped food, drinks and tobacco and had a friendly meal.

When it got dark, the men went back to their trenches calling 'Merry Christmas', 'Joyeux Nöel' and 'Fröhliche Weihnachten' to each other.

On Boxing Day they were fighting once more. There were three more Christmases during the war, but the soldiers never again made friends on Christmas Day.

Guzzling Guests

Can you spot -

- A soldier decorating a Xmas tree
- Three soldiers singing carols
- A soldier kicking a football
- 14 rats

Menu

Can you find -

- A soldier with 4 sausages
- 2 dogs carrying cans of soup
- 1 Xmas pudding
- a pot of tea

Bread was the main food of the Ancient ▲ Egyptians and every house had a bread oven like this one. It was heated by a charcoal fire. Bread was baked in moulds inside the oven or made into flat loaves and placed on the outside of it.

▲ **S**tone Age people cooked their meat in two ways. The simplest method was to roast it over a fire. To boil meat they filled a wooden or stone trough with water, then wrapped the meat in straw and put it in the trough. Next they heated the water by dropping in red-hot stones. A large joint of meat would be ready to eat in four hours.

▲ **T**hese oddly shaped pots were used to store food in an Ancient Greek kitchen. They held wine, olive oil, fish sauce and vinegar. The pointed ends of the pots fitted into holes in the kitchen floor.

This ingenious heater provided hot water for a Roman kitchen. The fire was fuelled by charcoal. ▶

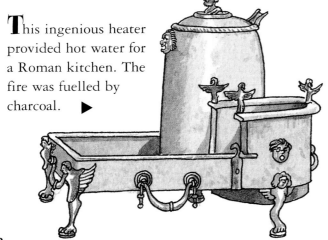

▲ **T**his great spit was in the kitchen of a medieval castle. It could roast the largest joints of meat. The meat was continually turned so it cooked evenly. This spit was worked by a dog running on a treadmill.

◀ **K**itchen ranges like this were common all over Europe by the 1700s. There is an oven to the left of the fire and a clockwork mechanism to turn the spit. Can you see the bellows used to fan the fire and the crane used to hang a cauldron over it?

Kitchens on wheels like this were used by armies about 100 years ago. Food was cooked while on the move so the soldiers could have a hot meal as soon as they had finished their day's march. ▶

Nineteenth-century inventors made many ingenious machines to make work in the kitchen easier. They were powered by steam or clockwork as there was no electricity then. This kitchen stove not only cooked meals but also made enough steam to power a sewing machine. ▼

Electric cookers became common in the 1950s. They were clean, didn't smell and heated up as soon as they were turned on. This model dates from 1951. It has a kettle-plug attachment on the side. ▲

Glossary

Acrobat — a person who performs gymnastic tricks

Altar — in ancient times, a place (usually a kind of table) where animals were killed as gifts to the gods

Bellows — an instrument for blowing air onto a fire

Carcass — the body of a dead animal

Cauldron — a large pot used for boiling food

Chariot — a two or four-wheeled vehicle used in ancient times, usually drawn by four horses

Discus — a heavy, flat disc thrown by athletes in competitions

Fakir — a hindu religious man

Gladiator — a trained fighter who fought with other men or animals in Ancient Roman arenas

Intestine — a long, coiled tube inside our bodies that digests food

Jaguar — a large, fierce cat that lives mostly in South American forests. It has black spots on its fur

Mutton — the meat from sheep

Ox — another name for a cow or bull

Pomegranate — a large orange-coloured fruit which is hard on the outside, and red and pulpy on the inside

Raja — an Indian prince or nobleman

Shaman — someone with special powers to communicate with the spirits and cure sickness

Spit — a narrow metal bar on which meat is roasted

Tapestry — a decorative cloth woven with pictures or patterns

Treadmill — a wheel turned by the weight of people or animals walking on steps inside it

Trencher — a large plate usually made of bread or wood

Trotters — another name for pigs' hooves. Each one has two large toes in the centre

Venison — the meat from deer

Vulture — a large, black bird that feeds on dead animals

Index